# Power of Now: Mindfulness, Living in the Moment and Creating the Future that You Want

By

## JOSE MARTINEZ

## Description

The power of now is a mindful approach towards living in the moment. The power of now will reveal to you how you can subdue the pain, stress, and anxiety that everyday struggles imposed on your mental and psychological wellbeing. The power of now, will help balance your life by subduing the thoughts of your past and the future and focusing on the present moment which itself is the truest path to being happy, mindful, enlightened, and creating the future that you want.

This book has been written and arranged to educate, and inform those that are still belong held back by the failures of their past, and those who want to become mindful of the present in order to harness the power of now, to better their present and future. You need to be guided by simple principles in order to optimize the power of now, in your lifestyle. When you become mindful, you will be able to free yourself from your past toxic beliefs and thoughts, and then harness your inner capabilities, in order to rewrite your present and future story.  Some of the things you will learn from this eBook include;

- The attitude that can help you become mindful and acquire the power of now!

- Mindful exercises that has been proven to increase the power of Now!

- Learning to live in the moment- the process

- Step by step guide on interpreting your thoughts and replacing negative thoughts with positive ones in order to regain control of your sub-conscious mind.

- Using your power of mindfulness in your daily living and difficult situations.

# Table of Content

# Conclusion

# Introduction

You might have heard about mindfulness but you don't have any clue about how to get started. You want to achieve a greater inner peace, enhance your focus and clarity, but you are quite unsure of those necessary steps that will get you there. You don't have to worry, every great achievement starts from somewhere, and the most important decision you have made is stepping into the right path towards attaining the power of Now!

Simply put, mindfulness is regarded as a time-sensitive way of boosting your wellbeing, happiness as well as sense of fulfilment. When you live in the power of now or when you are mindful, you will naturally become more empowered to do away with depression, anger, anxiety, pain and even drug abuse.

The ancient practice of mindful was believed to have originated in India some 2,500 years ago, where it was an entity of the re-awakening process in Hindu, Islam and Buddha practices. Though, Meditation originated from ancient practices, but the components of the practices have been adapted to deal with many modern challenges faced in the world today.

Have you ever sat down and felt upset by what someone said to you few weeks or even years ago? Have you ever paused suddenly and started feeling anxious about a meeting you will face in few days' time? All these are signs that you are not being mindful and you have not embraced the power of now! Realistically, anxiety, fear and worries do not solve issues, rather they make it appear bigger than they are actually are.

So, you may be asking yourself the question; what does it mean to be mindful?

Mindfulness means "paying attention". As a little child, your parents must have told you "mind your manners" several times, what they were actually telling you is that you must be mindful of the situation around you so that you wouldn't hurt anyone with your absent-mindedness.

Sometimes, being mindful may not be easy, especially when your thoughts are just running out of control as a result of a terminal disease you are suffering, or an emotional trauma you are passing through. Mindfulness will help you in these situations. Most of the problems that take control of our minds, emanated either from the past or from worries about the future. When you start practicing the act of mindfulness, you will start witnessing a higher level of energy that will help you achieve more in the present.

Anxiety, fear and depression occur when you replay your past experiences, and much of your thinking are supposed to be in the present, if you want to be successful. By moving your life more into the present, you will relate with your past and the future in a different and more proactive ways. This means those habitual thinking of the past will gradually fade away and they will eventually become less insistent and your mind will become clearer.

Mindfulness starts with paying attention to those little things happening around you, it may be the sound of the birds, the appearance of a new blooming flower, and the new opportunities that suddenly show up right in the middle of the chaos. The most beautiful sensations always reside in the present.

By practicing mindful exercises such as breathing, you will become more aware of the happenings around you, hence you will spend more time and focus on your present and not your past!

Once your habitual thinking begins to fade, your brain becomes more creative, especially at solving problems.

## Chapter 1

## What is Mindfulness and What Are Its Benefits?

Mindfulness can be described as the state of being conscious of something or a situation. It can be said to be that mental state of concentrating one's awareness on the present moment. It also involves the individual accepting his or her present thoughts, feelings, and sensations, for the purpose of achieving a peaceful inner state of mind.

Mindfulness can be regarded as a long term therapeutic technique that heals the body, mind and soul, and it offers the following benefits;

#1: self-control and objectivity

People who are ruled by thoughts of their past mistakes and failures do not possess enough self-will or self-control that can liberate them from such past problems. When you achieve the power of now, you will learn to control your thoughts, which means you will become more objective and more rational in the way you think.

#2: Tolerance

It is very easy to spot people who are mindful of what they do- they are highly tolerant, not because they are weak, nor timid, they have mastered the act of accommodating people for who they are without judging them hastily. When you are mindful of a situation, you want to give people the benefit of doubt, and you don't just accept any belief someone else is trying to impose on you.

#3: Enhanced flexibility

Those who live in the moment are flexible enough to understand that their past errors should not determine future successes. They are opened to new ideas and new possibilities, and that is why they make each moment in the present count, towards achieving a greater goal and objective.

#4: Improved mental clarity

When you are mindful, you will be able to investigate every beliefs and thoughts and you only want to stick to the truth. People's opinions about you will always be bias because nobody knows you better than you do, hence you will consider all judgments passed on you are then find out which one is actually true and the ones that are based on other people's imagination or thoughts about you. Mental clarity is directly attached to improved concentration or enhanced focus.

#5: Drastic reduction of psychological and mental stress within a short period of time

Mindfulness is the most potent element to fighting stress in whatever form. According to researchers, mindfulness is the most potent power that can promote adaptive response to stress triggers. Another research indicates that mindfulness does not take the "avoidance" approach to problems, rather, it helps an individual develop a "coping" method through self-affirmation and visualization techniques of resolving problems.

Lack of sleep, low energy, agitation, irritability, and having difficulty in concentrating, are just few of the symptoms of stress and anxiety that meditation can help deal with effectively.

#6: Enhance cognitive powers and ability to deal with illnesses

Those who suffer from terminal illnesses can rely on the power of being mindful to cope with such. Mindfulness may not take away symptoms of chronic illnesses but can make such illnesses become more manageable. Mindfulness can help you induce a state of relaxation for the brain and the body as a whole- this will lead to better brain functioning, as well as increased in the strength of your immunity. With higher brain functioning, there will be increase in awareness, and ability to feel connected on any situation.

#7: Mindfulness speeds up recovery

Mindfulness will not only help you cope with an illness and enhance your brain power, it will also recover quickly from a life-threatening event. It can be extremely painful to cope with the loss of a loved one, especially a family member or colleague, but when you have developed the act of being mindful, your mind will speedily get over such losses or event. Post-traumatic stress is toxic development that must be dealt with at all cost, and the best way to go about it is to take complete control of your conscious and sub-conscious mind. When you are in charge of your own mind, you delete harmful thoughts and replace them with good memories.

#8: Improved academic performance

Adults are not the only ones who benefit from being mindful, high school and college students can boost their academic performance tremendously by eliminating distractions and taking complete control of their own minds. When a student starts practicing mindfulness techniques, he or she will begin to regulate their emotions much better, likewise, he or she will start to develop creativity and problem-solving skills- all these can combine together to enhance academic performance on the long run.

#9: Mindfulness boosts resilience and perseverance

There is no situation you can't survive if you persevere. The reason why we make mistakes continuously is because we don't take our time to study a situation before responding. Mindfulness will improve your emotional regulation as well as empathy, confidence, mood and self-esteem.

Resilience is a skill that will help you cope with daily struggles. There are mindfulness techniques that will be explained in subsequent chapters that will help you control your emotions (resilience). Resilience can be a cognitive therapy that children can also learn.

#10: It improves workplace efficiencies

Mindfulness can make a huge impact on workplace performance. Being mindful in the work workplace means less mistake, more focus and more capabilities. As work-related stress is reduced, there are greater job satisfaction levels. Aside the enhanced work performance, mindfulness can increase productivity levels by reducing stress, fatigue and work-related depression- this means that more tasks can be completed within a short period of time.

There are countless other benefits one can derive from being mindful and living in the moment, all these hidden benefits will eventually show up as you continue to immerse yourself in mindfulness techniques.

## Chapter 2

### The 8 Attitudes That Defines a Mindful Heart.

As a beginner in mindfulness practice, you may be thinking that being mindful is a difficult step to take, but in actual sense, it is not. Even if you are unsure about how to proceed, you can start by learning about the attitudes that will define a mindful heart.

Just before mindfulness practices, it is important to know the concept behind mindfulness and what it means to be a mindful person especially when you are making extra efforts toward personal growth. The eight attitudes that that will contribute towards a flourishing mind, and personal growth are;

#1: A curious mind- You need to see things as a visitor, in a foreign land, this means you are curious about all beliefs and why an unpleasant situation has stuck to your mind. You need to see each situation as new and you are willing to investigate the situation to know if it is good for you to embrace or discard.

#2: A Non-judgmental mind- a mindful person is impartial, and doesn't label a person or situation as good or bad, right or wrong until they have completed their own investigation and thoroughly understand the person, situation or things. A mindful person will simply allow a situation to be.

#3: Acknowledges – a mindful person will recognize things as they are.

#4: Settled heart- A mindful person is comfortable in the moment and has contentment.

#5: Composure- A mindful person is composed, he or she remains in control with great insight and compassion.

#6: He lets things be- A mindful person does not feel the need to change everything. He lets things be with no need to force things to change in his or her favor.

#7: He is self-reliant – He makes decisions based on his or her own experiences and understanding. He or she knows what is true and what is not, hence he makes a decision based on thorough investigation of situations.

#8: He is self-compassionate – a mindful person does not indulge in self-reproach, he loves himself as he is with no criticism.

Now that you are aware of the attitude of a mindful person, these are the attitudes you must endeavor to cultivate because they form the basis of living in the moment and acquiring the power of Now!

As a mindful person the way you react to a situation must be positive, those who react negatively to situations often find themselves enmeshed in bigger problems that can break them and make them lose total control. If you can develop the highlighted mindful attitudes above, your life and lives of the people around you will be better off.

**What are the attitudes that will aid your Mindfulness practices?**

If you want to be successful, you need to allow it to happen, which means, your entire being must be brought into the techniques. Your attitude towards mindfulness techniques is very essential it is simply the "fertile soil" where you want to cultivate that power of Now! That is, the ability to bring your mind to calmness, relaxation, and improve your capabilities to see more clearly. The following attitudes have been found to increase your success rates in mindfulness practices;

- The beginner's mind,

- Patience,

- Persistence,

- Non-striving,

- Self-assurance or self-trust,

- Letting-it-go, and

- Acceptance.

#1: The Beginner's mind- This attitude is the one in which you believe a situation is new, even if you are familiar with it. For instance, "I have been enjoying this crunchy cereal mix for a while, maybe the taste will be different today". Having a beginner's mind is very important because it can help you get that freshness of breath over and over again. It is an attitude that raises your optimism and help you approach a situation more effectively.

#2: Patience- Patience is one of the fruits of wisdom, it is the ability to resist the urge to rush through the moment and remain opened to each moment as they come by. When you are open to a new moment, you will explore its fullness and seize every opportunity that comes with it. When you are opened to the moment, you will completely believe that things will eventually un-fold with time. You may be thinking that your body's clock is ticking away, being patient means you will avoid errors that will lead you nowhere.

#3: Just like patience, persistence is another attitude that can greatly help you to become mindful of your thoughts and actions. When you are patient even through the darkest of times, you have the believe that the steps you take everyday will eventually bring you to the desired end you wished for yourself. Persistence simply means "to keep on going". Even if you have little benefits coming in, you need to stick to your practice of mindfulness because there will always be a big break and new discoveries in being persistent.

#4: Non-striving – striving is the process of struggling or trying too hard to achieve something, which is a complete opposite of non-striving. Humans do strive in different ways, we want to please others by looking like them, we strive to become more relaxed, and we even strive too hard to make more money. It is important to remember while we are striving that the only thing we should do is to become mindful of the results we are getting, and then return to the main focus of our ambition or practice especially when we fail and realized that we have been distracted.

When you accept things as they are, you wouldn't strive too hard to please yourself or anyone else, you will become mindful and trust yourself more, while honoring your feelings.

#5: Acceptance is an attitude that can be described as the willingness to "let go". Acceptance does not mean you must settle for your current condition, neither does it mean you must accept injustice being meted to you. Acceptance simply means, you have come to understand why a situation is like that

## How to deal with the hindrances to mindfulness practices

Perhaps the best possible way to do away with all hindrances to mindful practices is to set out a regular mindfulness practice. You may want to start your mindfulness practices before your evening meals or just before you go for shower. Just make sure you stick to the schedule and to make it easier, you need to make use of the same place. Many people may think there are no clear ways of preventing old harmful thoughts from coming back, but in actual sense, they are the ones who are not willing to replace those thoughts with present realities.

The biggest obstacle to mindfulness perhaps, is having an idea of the right way to go about the mindful practices. Mindfulness techniques should make you feel more relaxed especially when you were initially stressed. When you are still feeling agitated during and after your mindfulness exercises, then you are probably doing it the wrong way.

That state of calmness remains one of the main benefits of mindfulness, it is important to note that we need to put our general mood into perspectives in order to be certain whether we have achieved calmness or not. You have not attained calmness when you feel relaxed but your old beliefs and thoughts are still in control.

Finding time for mindfulness exercises is another obstacle. Most people say they are too busy to find the time to practice meditation. When you are curious about mindfulness, you will definitely find time to indulge in its practice. You need to be clear about the steps to be taken during mindful practices, then you can slot in even few minutes a day to indulge in the exercises. Another option is to indulge in mindful practices at the end of the day when you are about to retire into your bed.

## Chapter 3

## Mindfulness Through Breath- First Step to Being Mindful.

Breathing as mindfulness practices are very helpful because; if you can control your breathing, you can start controlling the way you react to situations around you. The mindfulness practice of breathing means; to observe and be mindful of your breathing patterns.

It means you choose a breathing cycle and then pay attention to it as fully as you can. You may want to vary the time it takes for a breath as it moves through your nostrils, likewise, you can vary the contraction / expansion of the abdomen and chest while you perform the breathing exercises. Keep in mind that the objective here is to observe your everyday sensation. At the beginning of the breathing exercise, you may be distracted, for instance by the sounds emanating nearby (sounds of television, or people), hence you should consider choosing a quiet place to perform your mindful breathing exercises.

You need to be aware of your breathing when performing these exercises, that is why you should try and maintain focus and prevent any thought from interfering with your breathing cycles. If a thought forces itself into this exercise, you must guide the attention back to the breathing activities.

Just like in other forms of mindfulness exercises, the first part is to be aware of the present circumstances or present moment, and the second part is to accept that your mind will wander from the moment occasionally and there is no need to judge the thoughts even if it is a "negative one"- the objective is to guide your thoughts back to the exercise you are performing.

One thing you will notice if your mindful breathing exercises are effective is that the number of distracting thoughts will reduce gradually as you repeat the breathing exercises, because you are now being empowered to focus on the moment.

You may be asking yourself the question; what is so special about mindful breathing exercise? The answer is simple- it helps you focus on one thing at a time and not several thoughts trying to distract you.

Breathing exercises can be an indication of our stress level- if you find it difficult to focus on one thing (such as the air blasting your face or a bird flying in the sky), it means your stress level is high and you may not be able to maintain direct focus.

The good thing about the mindful breathing exercises is that you can observe it at any time of the day, whether you are in the supermarket, even in the traffic or work place. One thing you should learn is that, as you let the thoughts go, you will be able to let distracting thoughts go. The ability to let go off your breath also means you are learning to let an emotion run its course without holding on to it. Mindful breathing exercises are very helpful for those suffering from depression, caused by repetition of certain thoughts and emotions on daily basis.

### Simple steps to mindful breathing

Step #1: Take an erect and comfortable posture and close your eyes gently.

Step #2: bring your focus and attention to the floor you stand or sit on and for a few minutes, explore the sensations at the contact between your body and the floor.

Step #3: Bring your mind or awareness to the fluctuating patterns of sensations between your body and the floor surface (for instance, is it getting warmer or colder?), and breathe in and out.

Step #4: Shift your focus from the floor and place a hand on your abdomen as you breath in and out – feel the physical sensations emanating from your abdominal walls. As each breathe stretches your abdomen, make sure you pay careful attention and adjust the speed of your breathing occasionally. At this stage, your mind is totally aware of your breathing pattern and not the physical sensations between your body and the floor.

You may want to shift attention away from your breathing pattern, back to the sensations between your body and the floor, just make sure you ignore the thoughts of the stretching of your abdomen.

### Advance mindful breathing exercises

### #1: The Rhythmic breathing for concentration

While you settle for this breathing exercise, you need to perform the following steps

Step #1: Relax yourself into a full and relaxed rhythmic breathing just before you start your breathing practices. Keep in mind that the quality of your breathing will depend on the quality of your preparedness and practice steps.

Step #2: As a beginner, your breathing may still be controlled by the tension remaining in your body, and your initial regular patterns, but don't worry, you will get over such obstacles. Make sure you attain a state where your breathing comes in and out smoothly (you can maintain a rhythmic patter of 2-3 seconds breathe in and 2-3 seconds breathe out.

Step #3: Do not force this procedure, if you do, you will create another form of tensed state, hence you may end up distracting yourself from the exercise.

Step #4: Repeat this exercise until you are able to maintain a steady time space between breathing in and out without losing concentration.

### #2 Breath stretching

You need to learn to stretch your breath during mindful breathing practices, and the reason being that it will help you relax even more, and you will be able to commit yourself even more to other mindful activities.

Step #1: To start your breathing stretching exercise, simply start by inhaling and count slowly, numbers 1-6, hold your breath at 3 and then exhale at 6, then hold at 2 before exhaling at 4. Repeat this step.

Step #2: If you feel you are short of breath, simply let the breathing pattern go until you become comfortable, and then return to breath-holding step above.

Step #3: As the breath-holding become easier, you can increase it to a count of 8, 10 and so on, and make sure you hold on the half the counts (for instance, hold at 4, 5 and so on).

Step #4: once you have worked your breathe for about 10 minutes, you can then relax into your normal breathing ways.

### #3: Mind settling exercises

Getting your mind settled through breathing techniques, is one of the most important steps you must take if you want to live in the present moment. One of the main principles of mindful breathing is that if your focus remains scattered then your energy will be scattered.

Settling the mind will not only help you achieve new skills, it will also help you bring your blood pressure and stress levels under control, thus prolonging your life.

Step #1: Do not try to force your mind to be silent, you will end up adding more pressure and create tension. Instead you should watch out for silence underneath the noises generated by the daily random thoughts.

Step #2: Pay more attention to your breathing rate.

Step #3: As new thought begins to come up, focus more on your breathing patterns, no matter how prevalent such thoughts are. As you gradually return your focus to your breathe, you will gain more control of your mind, and this will force your mind to become quieter.

#### #4: Body relaxation

Body relaxation techniques are key to healthier body, likewise they help you develop better skills in handling other mindful techniques. Body relaxation is part of mindful mental practices; however, you can practice them along with your breathing exercises.

Step #1: Examine yourself from head to toe and release tension gently as you do so.

Step #2: Repeat the first step three times.

Step #3: Make sure each and every part of your body feel at ease and heavy and never stay rigid and tensed up. Make sure all muscle anxiety dissipates gradually as you repeat the steps, and let your body feel like you are sinking into the ground.

Just like any other practice in Mindfulness, breathing techniques must be practiced on daily basis, until you incorporate the idea into your daily lifestyle. When you take a deep breath before you react to an unpleasant situation, there are possibilities that you will make a more rational decision that wouldn't hurt your feelings later on.

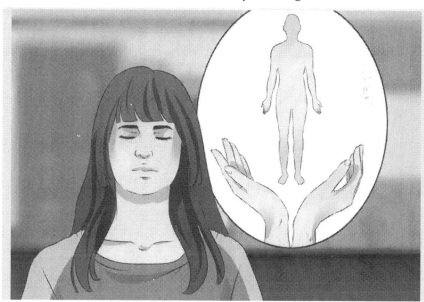

### #5: Create a unison between your breathing and movements

Qigong is best achieved when there is unison between your movements and breathing patterns. Unless you are otherwise instructed for certain movements, you must ensure that you maintain a deep, relaxed and eve breathing patterns. Since movements and breathe are linked, you must take the movements slow while you maintain the deeply-rooted relaxation.

In summary, mindful breathing exercises will help you observe some sensations that are connected to your breathing patterns. For instance, the rise and collapse of your abdomen while you inhale and exhale will help you prevent distractions and get immersed in the moment.

When you use equal breathing timing, you will be able to calm your mind even when there are racing thoughts getting out of control in your mind. Mindful breathing can also be very helpful when it becomes difficult to get some sleep.

## Chapter 4

## Step 2: Mindfulness Exercises Through Relaxation and Efforts.

Mindfulness through effort simply means, doing what you have to do. While some people do possess lots of energy, and they are always on the move, in search of what to do, others will require some "push" or assistance, just to get going. In meditation, you just don't seek what to do, rather, just to escape, rather you are developing some efforts internally. It means observing your mind and then concentrating on a subject matter.

There is a believe that putting too much effort will make you restless, and putting too little effort will make you dull. In mindfulness, the state of your body and the mind are definitely a measure of your effort. If you are unsure about how to start a mindfulness exercise for relaxation and effort, have a stand on your feet, then align your body by pulling out your chest and then make your spine straight.

#1: The sitting posture

This is perhaps the commonest mindfulness posture exercise you need to learn. When done repeatedly, the sitting posture exercise will definitely improve your overall posture and thus boosting your feeling of confidence.

Step #1: Sit uprightly on a chair with your feet on the ground and your back rested on the seat.

Step #2: Allow your legs to be separated.

Step #3: Make sure your torso is located at right angle to your thigh.

Step #4: close your mouth and eyes in order to rest them during this exercise, and don't try to force a smile, rather allow your mouth to take its natural shape.

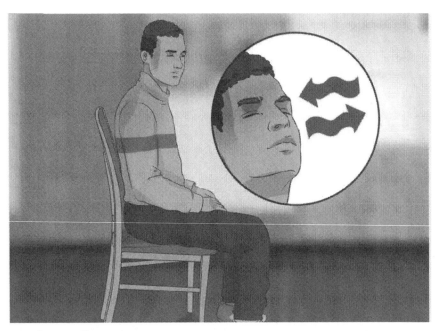

## #2: The standing posture

The standing posture is a mindfulness posture that you can practice at any time of the day. The standing posture is also important because it is the foundation for many other postures, likewise, it will promote your overall wellbeing and confidence.

Step #1: stand upright and let your feet to remain parallel and must be separated by shoulder width.

Step #2: slightly allow your knees to bend.

Step#3: Gently raise your arms to a level where your hands become even or slightly lowered below your shoulders.

Step #4: allow your elbows to bend slightly.

Step #5: Let your hands remain at one-foot length apart, while your palms are pointing downwards.

Step #6: Let your fingers slightly curved and separated, while pretending that you are holding a ball in your hand in a relaxed way.

Step #7: Just like you did in the sitting posture, allow your eyes and mouth to remain closed in an unforced natural way.

Step #8: Remain in this position for about 5 minutes and then relax for about 15 seconds before repeating the position. You can perform between 3 and 5 repetitions at a time.

## #3 The walking posture

You can practice the walking posture in your spare time, and it is a posture that will help you remain relaxed even when you are walking. Keep in mind that the walking posture will require a larger practice space than the sitting posture, hence you must plan accordingly.

Step #1: Make sure your foot is lifted with your heel first.

Step #2: Take a step forward with your left foot first.

Step #3: Let your body and hands sway in the right way while you move.

Step #4: Only step your right food forward after your left has been completely placed on the ground.

Step#5: You can repeat this step for about 25 minutes or longer.

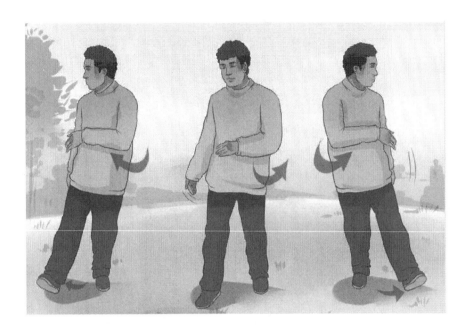

## #4: Other basic postures

There are several other postures you can try out aside the sitting, standing and walking postures in mindfulness. Always keep in mind that the different postures you practice will focus on different parts of the body, likewise you can use them to hone diverse mental techniques that can promote your spiritual awareness. Do not forget that all these techniques will demand your previous breathing, mental, and relaxation skills.

• The Supine posture- This posture requires that you lay down. Make sure you lay on your back while allowing your legs to stay straight, with your arms staying straight by your side. This is one of the postures intended to enhance body relaxation.

• The sideways lying - To perform this posture, simply lay on your side, while keeping the upper body straight. Make sure your legs are bent slightly, and then place the upper hand gently on your hip while your lower hand is placed by the head. This posture practice is intended to relax your body and mind.

• The Half Lotus posture- To practice this posture, you will have to sit up while you allow your left foot to rest on your right thigh (this should be under the left knee), and make sure your hands are rested on your knees. This posture will help stretch your lower body and legs.

- The cross-legged posture – You need to sit upright to perform this posture. Cross your legs, while resting your hands in front of your stomach. This posture will help in stretching your legs and you will become relaxed.

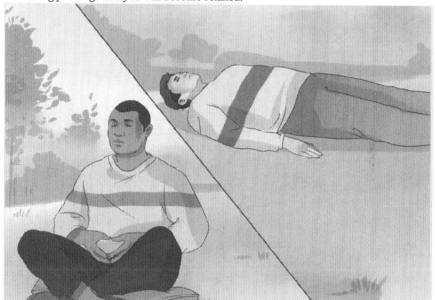

**Chapter 5**

**Step 3: Living in The Moment and Achieving Your Goals**

If you are struggling to attain your personal goals and objectives, you may want to learn how the power of living in the moment can make a significant impact in achieving such goals. The most important thing you should know is that, if you are not happy in the present moment, then your future goals and objectives will remain a mirage.

Mindfulness is that state of awareness and attention to the present events, it means you are open and accept the present. Oftentimes, our everyday behavior does not reflect the goals and objectives we have set for ourselves. If you are unclear about your values, you may wander off you're your purpose and that will bring unnecessary sufferings.

If you want to use the power of now to achieve your goals, then you need set realistic goals that are in tune with the moment, and then set detailed objectives and goals for your future based on what you are doing in the present moment. Live within the moment because that is the only one you can control and as you begin to take control of the moment, the future will eventually play according to your tunes and you will be happy with the goals you have achieved.

There are 6 basic tools you can use to achieve your goals through mindfulness and the power of Now!

- Clarity

- Focus

- Internal motivation

- Gradual control and change of thoughts and behavior,

- Observation of thoughts, and

- Embracing the unpleasant.

#1: Clarity- You need to know exactly what you want or what you are aiming for and the changes you are expecting right at the moment. Lack of clarity can be caused by a number of factors and one of such is the fact that you are bothered by people's opinions about you or past beliefs and culture that place limitations on you. Without clarity, you cannot live in the moment and harness the power of now, which means your goals will remain unclear.

#2: Focus- Focus on the moment. If you don't get it right in the present moment, your future goals cannot be fulfilled. Focus on putting all your efforts and concentration on what you are doing right now. If you are mindful of the moment, you will make less mistakes, and achieve your goals in bits. The negative thinking that derail goals are mere distractions, and the only way you can allow them is to allow your mind to wander to your past and the future.

#3: Internal motivation- It can be difficult to live in the moment when you are not motivated well enough. The best possible way to develop internal motivation is to have an understanding why your goal and objectives are important to you deep into your core. This is not about the extrinsic rewards you are expecting.

#4: Gradual control and change of thoughts and behavior – we hardly make progress when we are still being held captive by the thoughts of the past. Except your current thoughts and behavior are making you to achieve positive results, you need to gain control of your thoughts and behavior.

Most of the past thoughts are controlled by your un-conscious mind and that is why they are difficult to get rid of. Fortunately, the thoughts that you allow to influence your current state of mind will eventually control your conscious mind. If you want to change your thoughts, start replacing the old limiting thoughts and behavior with new, motivating and enthusiastic thoughts and behavior. It wouldn't take long until the old thoughts are completely replaced by new, motivating thoughts. As your thinking patterns change gradually, you will start unleashing the power of the moment and your happiness and goals will eventually become more evident.

#5: Observation of thoughts- You don't have to fight with negative thoughts all the time, you can allow them to float, but don't give them the power to get in-between you are your long-term goals. Observing your thoughts will help you live in the present moment where past and future thoughts will not gain upper hand over you. Observing your thoughts will even become much easier when your sub-conscious mind is completely under your control.

#6: Embracing the unpleasant – The most successful people who understand that negative experiences are part of life, have decided to develop plans to overcome such unpleasant experiences. Embracing the unpleasant can help you achieve your long-term goals because the unpleasant experiences will not deter you from following up your dreams.

Learning to embrace the unpleasant means you will be able to embrace your challenges in education, health, career, relationships and even parenting. When you understand the power of now, you will develop a resistance against the influence of negativities. Your values will be your guide as well as the stepping stones toward the moves you make in life. You may want to choose a mentor who will identify those patterns of behavior that are in tune with your goals and objectives. Your mentor will be in a better position to hold accountable when your behavioral patterns are not in conformity with your aspirations.

These tools highlighted above have been found to be effective in helping you become mindful of the present moment and embrace the power of now!

# Chapter 6

## Step 4: How to Practice Mindfulness in Your Daily Life: Living in the Moment

Regardless of how busy your life is, you need to incorporate mindfulness if you want to unleash the power of now, and achieve your goals. From playing to working, school, cooking and even checking your emails and smartphone messages, you need to stay mindful in order to remove those feelings of anxiety, and panic.

Do not live your life like an auto-pilot, you need to take pleasure and cognizance of every step you take. Here are some tips on how you can practice mindfulness in your everyday life, in order to become happier, and achieve your goals and objectives.

With mindfulness, you must be present in each moment and you must be aware of yourself as well as your surroundings and your feelings- this is when you will have the full potential to use the power of now to make rational decisions. When you are mindful of the moment, will be able to compose yourself and remain calm and with the abundance of every moment, your senses will become alert and your mind will be inspired by each breath you take in each moment.

So how can you practice mindfulness from day to day?

Most people think that true mindfulness is practiced by the Buddhist and Hindu monks, but in actual sense, everyone can become mindful because it helps to ward off distractions. There are numerous ways through which you can incorporate mindfulness to your everyday affair. Your mind will always be with you, what you need to do is make the mind aware of your immediate situation. Here are some of the ways through which you can become mindful in each moment;

#1: when you wake in the morning, just take few minutes to breathe deeply through regulated inhalation and exhalation. Pay attention to any sound, or smell that you have not noticed before you begin the mindful exercise. Make sure your body remains still for the moment you are inhaling and exhaling.

#2: Create and write down the things you are grateful for, and make sure you remind yourself every morning about these things- these will eventually replace negative thoughts and the thought of your needs and inadequacies.

#3: Make sure you are aware of your breathe. Know the times when you breathe deeply and the period your breath is shallow. Situations that cause you to breathe deeply are pleasant situations you must be mindful of, then you need to learn to live in the moment by learning to breathe deeply and smoothly. If you are effective in paying attention to the way you inhale and exhale then you are being mindful of the moment.

#4: In those moments when you are impatient and anxious, you need to pay attention to your breathing and bring it under control. If you are stuck in the long traffic or waiting in line inside a shopping mall, just calm down and start counting your breathe instead of being mindful of the situation. As you create a balance between inhaling and exhaling, you will find yourself feeling more in control of the situation. Instead of becoming upset, you need to see every opportunity as a chance to become mindful, therefore, taking charge of your breathing will naturally make you become calmer.

You can only achieve your everyday goal when you are calmer and you can control your breathe and your actions, every single second. If you can be mindful of your breathe, then you can achieve your tasks at work and avoid procrastination.

#5: Commit yourself to 15-minutes of sitting still and remain still, on daily basis. You can make use of a timer to achieve this purpose, where you can sit somewhere comfortably and then observe each thought within, as they pass move through your mind. You need to be aware of each thought and as they pass through your mind, let these thoughts pass and do not pass any judgment. As your thought floats, consider the ones that are unpleasant and then replace them with pleasant thoughts. As the pleasant thoughts become stronger, they will eventually overrule the unpleasant thoughts and that is how you become motivated to achieve even more positive things, toward the fulfilment of your goals.

#6: Continue to practice mindfulness techniques during routine activities.

Though, these tips may be very challenging in the first few days of practice, but the more you stay with them, the more clarity you will achieve towards achieving your goals. You will also establish a strong connection between your body, mind and spirit, and that connection will bring you into the fulfilment of your life's goals.

## Chapter 7

### Visualization Techniques for Being Mindful- Living in The Moment and Creating the Future That You Want.

### Visualization techniques

Now that you know about the secrets and laws of attraction through the use of Visualization procedures, you need to keep in mind that you need to fix your mind first, before you can use your power of imagination to attract success to yourself. Mind-fixing should be gradual because it helps you eliminating the past negative thoughts while you focus on more positive thoughts.

Before you believe in your goal, you need to have an idea of what exactly it looks like. You just need to see it before you believe it. Visualization helps you create a mental image of future events you want in your life, when you visualize a desired outcome, you have a glimpse of its eventuality, and are motivated to pursue the goal. Through visualization you can create your desired future. Visualization should not be seen as a gimmick rather it is a well-developed method for improving your performance towards achieving your goals and desires.

Visualization Techniques steps

**Imagination-** Draw a realistic plan for yourself and break them into smaller units that are achievable. Give yourself sufficient time-frame to achieve each stage in such a way that you don't place too much pressure on yourself.

**Coordination-** Coordination is a visualization technique that helps you reduce your fear and anxiety about achieving your future. The purpose of using coordination in Visualization is to achieve your goals by using the one-step-at-a-time approach. You don't have to rush through as most people want to, rather, take a simple and gradual approach.

**Concentration-** this steps allows you to follow your dreams with poise, and perfection , without losing focus. Athletes for instance can make use of visualization techniques to increase their performances by focusing at breaking one record at a time- they tend to break their own records before attempting to break world records.

There are basically two types of visualization;

-Outcome visualization- this entails the envisioning of your goal, trough the creation of a mental image alongside the desired outcome by using all your senses. Make sure you hold on your mental image as close as possible, and when you imagine the satisfaction and excitement of making it to the finish line, you will be motivated to the end.

- Process Visualization is a type of visualization that allows you envision each of the necessary actions you must take to achieve the final results you want.

## Affirmations- what are they and how can you use them to enhance your self-esteem?

Simply put, affirmations are positive and negative statements that we speak by mouth or in our mind and we stick with these affirmations for the rest of our lives. Affirmations can simply be natural or automatic, and most times they are made on purpose. Affirmations may relate to some parts , present and the future. Some of the common affirmative statements used on general issues are;

- Oh, what a bright and beautiful morning!

- Most new movies are boring,

- Oh! I am finished!

These are just natural statements that simply show our feelings as we face different situations in life. Consider positive affirmations like the ones below;

-Every day I am stepping forward and forward!

-I will keep losing weight everyday until I weigh below 75 pounds!

-I am a money magnet, money is attracted to me in every way !

-I am healthy. I live my life to the fullest!

These are positive affirmations, and can also be regarded as statement of intent. These statements clearly reveal our desired future and they are statements that can change our lives for the better. The most wonderful things about these statements of intent is that the more we use them , the more they form part of our lives. They work like small pieces of rocks thrown into a pond, they build up gradually until they fill up the pond of water.

Your power of affirmation will only work when you say them and keep them in your mind for a very long time. You need to hold different thoughts in your heart and make force them into your mind until they replace the ones that were there before. You need to remember that each and everyone has a set of thoughts that occupies his or her mind on regular basis, and the thoughts that keep coming into our mind are influenced by many things, including social interactions, education, life experiences, family upbringing and many more. Low self-esteem victim, will natural harbour different thoughts that someone with high self-esteem.

If an average person wants to become successful, he needs to make positive affirmations like a successful person who has high self-esteem. Now the question is , how can I change my life my changing my thoughts  through high self-esteem ?

The answer is simple and straightforward.

You are in your present situation because you have been thinking in a certain way for long. As a result of this prolonged and stereotype thinking, some neural pathways have formed in your brain and when you keep finding yourself in certain bad situations the already formed neural pathway will keep bringing the already formed thoughts that will also initialize the same old actions that you have been taking to handle the situation. For this reason, nothing new may come out of your actions and you remain in the same state of mind.

When you change your thoughts abruptly, you create new neural pathways in your brain and these will correspond to new thoughts that will boost your self-esteem. For this reason, the brain does not automatically bring the old thoughts to the fore when old situations repeat themselves. When you change your thoughts and create new neural pathways in your brain, new thoughts will be produced in response to old situations. And new actions will be explored and then a new outcome will distinctly bring about new possibilities. With new possibilities, your self-esteem is boosted because you no longer see the old results you are used to. It takes a while for your brain to get use to this new situation but the more you change your old thoughts the more positive your life becomes.

In another way, your sub-conscious mind will find it extremely difficult to differentiate between imaginary and real things most times and this is why you suffer from low self-esteem (you believe that certain bad situations will always repeat themselves). After a while, your sub-conscious mind will start believing that imaginary things are real and when this feelings get stronger, it will match the inner scenario with the external one .

Changing your inner scenario gradually with affirmations and visualization techniques will eventually change your inner reality and when your inner reality is changed successfully, the outer one is eventually changed and that is when your self-esteem is boosted . With a higher self-esteem, you will start meeting new people and establishing long lasting relationships.

We are strengthened daily by our affirmations and visualization, and our beliefs are normally stored in our sub-conscious minds. The sub-conscious mind works like a computer, it takes an input and from that it gives an output. Even the bible says "Out of the abundance of heart, we speak", therefore you need to change your affirmations because they go beyond the reality of the present and creates new future through the words and actions we take right now.

### How to use your affirmations- the Dos and don'ts of Affirmation

#### • Always use the present tense and not the future tense

Do not use the future tense when using affirmation to boost your self-esteem. For instance don't make an affirmation like "I will be wealthy", the reason being that , your being wealthy will remain in the future forever.

The reason why you must use present tense is that your sub-conscious mind only brings about the command it is given , hence you must say "I am wealthy" or "I choose to be wealthy". Many psychologists believe that affirmative words such as "Choose" are always better and keep in mind that you can't jump into the future if your present is not ready for it.

- **Remain positive.**

Your sub-conscious mind is incapable of dealing with negative affirmations, and it only works on the laws of focus and growth only. When you feed your sub-conscious mind with positive thoughts, you affirmations continue to build your confidence in what you want to achieve, and the results will remain positive. Instead of making the affirmations "I am not fat", it is better you say "I am fit". The use of the word "Not" may be misinterpreted by your subconscious mind; therefore you must be straightforward positively.

- **Speak and write down your affirmations**

Your affirmations can either be written down or spoken, make sure you repeat saying them up to twenty times when you wake up in the morning or before you go to bed in the night. The more you repeat your affirmations on daily basis, the better. There are many affirmation practicing techniques, including the "Mirror technique" demonstrated by the world famous cartoonist- Scott Adams.

- **Repetition**

Repetition is the key to successfully using the power of affirmations. In order to create a significant change in your life while boosting your self-esteem, you need to use your affirmations several times a day till they eventually become a reality.

### The Mirror technique for self-esteem boosting through affirmations

The mirror technique is a self-help habit that can increase your self-esteem drastically within a short period of time. The Mirror technique is as follow;

Step 1: Stand in front of your mirror each morning and look straight into your eyes.

Step 2: Repeat the affirmations with guts, and put more energy as you repeat those words.

Looking into your own eyes through this technique will help you establish a strong connection between your subconscious minds and your eyes. You need to repeat this especially when you pass in front of the mirror, just stop and repeat the statements to boost your self-esteem. There are many psychologists and writers who can boast of the efficacy of this technique in restoring self-confidence.

### How does Visualization works in creating positive image?

Knowing the systematic ways through which visualization works will help you visualize much better. You must not apply a technique mindlessly, because it may not yield the desired result if you do so. Here is a simple explanation on how the technique called Visualization works and helps boost your self-esteem.

The mind comprises of two parts; the sub-conscious mind and the Conscious mind. The conscious mind is also referred to as the "Rational mind" and it is the one we use in thinking. When we repeatedly think about something, it sinks gradually into our sub-conscious mind, which is also referred to as the "Creative mind". Our sub-conscious mind is programmed like a computer, It simply does not think on its own, therefore it does not distinguishes between the good and bad or between the truth and false, however, it only takes the face value and accept whatever is delivered into it.

When you subconscious mind is fed the same thoughts over and over again, it will gradually take such thoughts seriously and work on bringing to thoughts into existence. The lifetime experiences we have are stored in our sub-conscious minds, where they are accessed often and when the subconscious mind brings about the situations for which our repetitive thoughts are revealed, then we suffer low self-esteem because we believe that whatever our subconscious mind says is what we must follow.

In order for you to understand how the visualization technique works, you need to understand that the only pre-eminent language of your sub-conscious mind is images. Even though, the sub-conscious mind understands words very well, it can be much more easily influenced by images. For this reason, virtualization is very effective in turning around your sub-conscious mind and makes it deliver whatever you want.

According to Peter McWilliams *"To visualize is to see what is not there, and what is not real-It is a dream. As a matter of fact, to visualize is simply to make visual lies , however, such lies have a way of coming true".*

In order to make visualization technique works for you, you must only visualize the expected end result and not the entire process of achieving success. You need to constantly remind your sub-conscious mind what you want and leave the rest for your sub-conscious mind to figure out how you will achieve such success.

### The rules of Visualization-How Visualization works to boost your self-esteem

The process of using virtualization techniques to boost your self-esteem will require 6 steps;

### Step #1: Set a goal for yourself

It is very important to send a message conveying your exact desires into your sub-conscious mind, and this is the reason why you need to set a goal. For instance, your car will not get fixed if you tell your auto-technician how fast your car can go or how much you bought it, instead of telling him the exact fault. If you want your subconscious mind to manifest wealth, you must tell it how much as well as the time you want it. Then you can visualize how you want to get this money (for instance, by cheque, or doing some legitimate extra jobs), and the time you want the money (for instance, before Christmas).

### Step #2: Always skip the details

In order to make visualization techniques work in boosting your self-esteem, you need to skip the details and focus on the desired end. Your sub-conscious mind simply understands the goal or the ultimate aim you plan to establish, and you must leave this to your sub-consciousness to handle. You need to have an image of the end result in your mind, and you will quickly realize that all necessary steps needed to make the goal become a reality will be taken care of. Whether you want to boost your self-esteem through a better health, more salaries or a bigger house, it all depends on creating that positive image for the sub-conscious mind.

### Step #3: Embrace clarity

Make sure the images you send to your sub-conscious mind are clear, concise and accurate. Make sure you put yourself into the entire image ( for instance, if your friend has a house that you admire so much, you need to create an image of yourself in that house to boost your self-confidence towards achieving it. If you continue to send an image of your friend in that house, into your sub-conscious mind, then you may never achieve it).

You need to know that your sub-conscious mind will only bring to the fore, those images you create within. If you want a better job, then create an image of yourself in a new office-this is one of the best possible ways of boosting your self-esteem at the long run. If you create an image of yourself in a better position, you may not necessary find a new job, but you may be promoted into a higher position earlier than you think.

### Step #4: Remain vivid about your images

Being vivid with the images you send to your sub-conscious mind simply means, adding some brightness and beauty unto your mental images. You need to understand that your sub-conscious mind finds it extremely difficult to differentiate between real things and imagine things , you can thus capitalize on this to create more realistic images because, the more realistic the images created are, the more impressed your sub-conscious mind becomes and the higher your self-esteem becomes.

### Step #5: Make use of the present realities

While learning the ways through visualization enhances your self-esteem, you need to understand that your sub-conscious mind only understands the present and not the past, therefore everything happens in the present. Your conscious mind is able to label an event or image as having happened last month, however, your subconscious mind relays what is happening presently, even though in reality it has happened before or you imagined it to be happening in the future.

### Step #6: Do not pass judgments

Since your subconscious mind is unable to differentiate between good or bad, however, your conscious mind is capable of differentiating the good from the bad. For instance, your sub-conscious mind does not understand whether it is good or bad to be obese, however your conscious mind makes you feel sad if you are obese. In order for your subconscious mind to help you, it simply observes the image you feed into it and then support it by influence the choices of foods you make. In order for your sub-conscious mind to maintain that physical image you think about, it must sustain some consistency with the mental image you supply, therefore the critical point of not passing judgment unto your sub-conscious mind, will help you feed more positive images into it.

## Chapter 8

### The Laws of Mindfulness You Must Obey to Achieve Your Goals, Remain Happy and Creating the Future That You Want!

**Law number 1: Do not bother yourself on how and when things will happen because it is of no use micro-managing the universe by dictating how your life should unfold.**

You need to realize that positive change will always come with a natural flow and contentment and it is your duty to be in consonance with the flow of life through consciously experiencing some clarity about your mission. Learn to listen and pay attention to everyone and everything happening around you. Do that which is fun, and do good to others, and this will ignite the law of attraction in you and your life's circumstances will be improved immensely.

**Law number 2: Access your true power of intention by bringing your attention to the spaces in-between your thoughts.**

One of the best possible ways of visualizing success is by filling up those empty spaces in-between your negative thoughts with your intentions and goals. When you allow a sense of intention move through your thoughts, you will start to gain power and control over your mind.

Learn to create a positive intention every day, because it will help you in every areas of your life. You can practice this by learning to do simple things such as "learning to walk up to the kitchen and wash all the dishes every morning" .

When you learn to create positive intentions every day, it will help you in reconnecting with your feelings and positive energy.  It is quite important that you realize that connecting with the intentions filled into the spaces between your thoughts will help you merge your energy and you will become more conscious of what you do. When you are conscious of your thoughts and actions, you can entertain positive thoughts, ideas, and feelings that can empower and uplift you.

Create intentions with your creative mind by taking simple steps at a time, for instance you can decide to type a professional CV today and then create an ad tomorrow, or even start a blog. By the time you realize it , your thoughts will be easily guided by positive intentions. You actions will bring about intentions , while your intentions will take you into a level of awareness. With this you will soon discover that the power of intention is spiritual.

A popular quote from Abraham Hicks states that *"The amount of time it takes you to get from where you are presently to where you want to be , is just the time it takes you to change the intention and vibration within you"* This simply means that you can achieve an instant manifestation of positivity when you change the vibration within you.

**Law number 3: Realize deep down in you that you possess the ability to attract whatever you want even when you have no idea about it**

Sometimes you can imagine or picture what you want but have no idea how to get it. Your first step towards the situation is to feel at peace with yourself, without putting any pressure to achieve it. Fighting your feelings wouldn't help, rather you should make peace with it.

The notion that you don't know or how to make something happens will always inhibit your power to be positive, and it can unconsciously narrow your focus. Pure acceptance is the way out of attracting peace of mind because it cuts through the thoughts of "I DON'T KNOW". You need to change the way you relate with "I don't know how" and you will soon discover that you actually know how when you feel your thoughts with positive intentions- there is a power that lies within intentions that automatically helps you know that which you do not.

Have you ever wondered how electricity and other elements were discovered? It wasn't as if scientists wanted to discover something, but their intentions were to create something and when they became proactive, they eventually stumbled on their discoveries.

**Law number 4: Gain the self-awareness of supreme powers within you**

If you believe you have a soul within you then you should consider the fact that there is something about you that is super-natural. Wanting something is not a creative energy, however realizing that you are more than ordinary will support some form of effortless manifestation of your goals. There is a part of you that constantly monitors how life changes regardless of your present circumstances. The supreme powers in you will remain fearful until you decide to activate them. The free, fearless and knowing powers in you will arise spontaneously when you recognize them.

Each human possesses some boundless, free and universal self, that reside within the heart and beyond body and mind. You need to trust the fact that there is more to you than you had thought, and until you give the power of creation some thought, you wouldn't discover its infinite powers.

**Law number 5: Pursue your joy and stay in the flow of synchronicity**

Consider the fact that those things in life that excite you the most will always come complete with all the tools that can support you in doing such things. When you synchronize yourself in those little things that brings you pleasure, you will easily achieve them. You can transfer this power into other things by acting on the opportunities within the situations you face every day.

It is important that you help the universe in manifesting certain things; hence you need to take some intuitive and guided actions. You can do this by staying still at first, and then act on the power of your happiness. Take some break often and let your power of intuition show you what to do. Taking intuitive and guided actions will help avoid certain mistakes that would have taken you longer time to achieve your aims and goals.

## Law number 6: Go for the essence of your desire and forget all distractions

Try this simple process right now – think of a goal you have, whisper it to yourself and ponder on its essence. If your goal is to have a partner this year, then your essence is definitely a partner. Pursuing your essence and forgetting about all distractions can help you stay focus.

The reality of the existence of your goal lies within you, but as humans, we get distracted easily when pursuing our goals. You need to understand that there is a point where each goal starts and ends, and there is a power in the first step you take towards achieving your goals and that first step determines how you finish. When you focus more on your goal, you attract all elements of success to yourself faster and the expected results is increased calm, and feeling of more power of control plus better clarity of your essence or goal.

## Law 7: The freedom of creating reality expands with your attention

Paying attention to the things you want will naturally bring more of that thing. According to Jane Roberts *"The hatred of war will not bring peace, only the love of peace will bring it"*.

Learn to practice that act of "feeling into" in that special goal or ambition by paying even the simplest attention to it. Let your attention fall upon your goal . Consider the fact that pure attention is as easy as looking into the eyes of a little infant. Paying attention is simply more of feeling than thought, hence when you allow such feelings to envelop you, you will become more aware of what you need to do to achieve your purpose. Those who pursue their dreams with strong feelings or passion often end up successful compare to those who bury themselves deep into their thoughts.

Burying yourself in the feeling of the end results of your goals will disrupt the old fashion thoughts and drive you into a new direction to achieve your goals and objectives. Regardless of the external circumstances you are facing, you can achieve your goal when you bury yourself in the feelings of your dreams.

## Law 8: Make use of affirmations and Visualizations in the most possible counter-intuitive ways

It is ideal to make use of affirmative actions and visualization techniques, but you need to consider the fact that your creative powers are far beyond your exercises, and techniques . Your creative powers work like the force of gravity, because they pull whatever you need unto you.

Make sure you are open to the automatic manifestation of your dreams and goals because it will set you free from your old thoughts. Learn to make your affirmations as if they have come to past, and are real. Learn to feel your inner strength when you tackle each stage in realizing your dreams, and when you do this, you will easily separate yourself rom doubts and set in motion the desire to fulfill your goals.

**Law 9: If you want to create a new thing, learn to get in the habits of recreating things you already have**

One of the best possible ways to use the power of virtualization is to recreate or reproduce what you already have. The act of creating something new out of what you have already is quite magical. Through feeling and visualizing, you can create something new and unique, this will definitely amplify your desire and focus and will even help you realize your new potentials and what you can achieve in the nearest future. Many successful entrepreneurs today did not create things that are 100% genuine, rather they brought a new dimension into an existing product, and their clients were able to see those new inventions.

**Law 10: Your life is a result of the things you think about more often**

There is no doubt about the fact that what you think about everyday will actually determine how well you live or how well you realize your dream. If you are skeptical, you will definitely achieve average results, and when you are optimistic, you will always end up achieving more positive results.

From a psychological perspective, there is a strong merit attached to this law of attraction. Your thoughts are simply magnetic, and as you think, your thoughts are sent to the external universe and they attract things that are on the same frequencies and whatever you sent to the universe will definitely return to their sources which is your mind.

Make sure you try as much as possible to clear your mind off negative thoughts. believe in your actions (speaking, acting, and thinking), as though you have already achieved them, and when you emit that frequencies of having achieved already what you ask for, then the energy of attraction moves around and move people, events, and circumstances in your favour.

Receiving is part of your thinking, and it is simply the way you feel once your goals and dreams have been manifested. The law states that, if you want to lose some weight for instance, you should rather focus on your perfect weight instead of focusing on losing weight. when you feel the feelings of your perfect weight, you will naturally summon that results to you because you will become motivated to achieve your desired weight loss. You need to keep in mind that it takes a while for the universe to manifest your desires.

## Conclusion

There is no better time to become mindful than now! The world around us is changing and only the smarter ones are catching up. You cannot boost your brain power and become smarter if you cannot become mindful. Being mindful is not a difficult task, it takes dedication and open-mindedness, and when you completely take charge of your own mind, you will be amazed at how much you can accomplished with it.

This book has given you enough information on how to become mindful and make use of the power of the moment, in order to create the future that you need. It is important that you make it your guide from day to day until you are able to use mindful practices from day to day.

Made in the USA
Middletown, DE
16 May 2018